CHIGWELL AND LOUGHTON
A Pictorial History

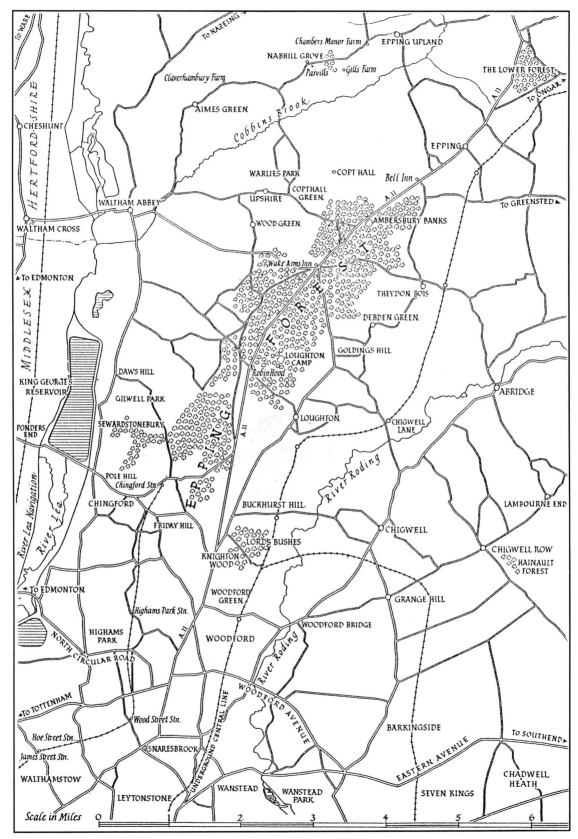

Map of the Chigwell and Loughton area in 1945.

CHIGWELL AND LOUGHTON
A Pictorial History

Stephen Pewsey

Phillimore

1995

Published by
PHILLIMORE & CO. LTD.
Shopwyke Manor Barn, Chichester, West Sussex

ISBN 0 85033 939 1

Printed and bound in Great Britain by
BIDDLES LTD.
Guildford, Surrey

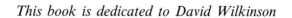

This book is dedicated to David Wilkinson

List of Illustrations

Frontispiece: Map of the Chigwell and Loughton area in 1945

Acknowledgements

This book would not have been possible without the help and advice of many people. I would like to thank in particular the staff of Loughton Library, especially Tom Holliday and Roy Cummings; the staff of Newham Museum Service (who curate the Essex Field Club Photographic Archive), especially Pat Wilkinson and Lesley Richardson; Jane Dansie of Essex County Libraries; Eddie Dare from the Chigwell and Loughton History Society for much valuable advice; and especially George Collins. For permission to use many of the photographs, I would like to thank Essex County Libraries, Newham Museum Service, Aerofilms, and last but certainly not least, Norman Jacobs.

Introduction

> Chigwell ... is generally regarded as one of the sweetest villages in the county. It abounds in beautiful woodland scenery, extending ... along the verge of the forest; and from Chigwell Row, which forms a neat little village of itself, a fine view opens over the county up to Danbury Church ... and along a great part of the Thames ... The parish is thickly studded with good mansions.

So wrote the historian D.W. Coller in 1861 in his *People's History of Essex*. Of Loughton, he wrote,

> Loughton is a large and delightful parish with a very picturesque village and ground of remarkably undulating character. The views and scenery in this village are equal to almost anything of the kind in this part of England.

Chigwell and Loughton, in the south-west corner of Essex, remain desirable places to live, and there may still be those who echo Dickens' striking claim, 'Chigwell, my dear fellow, is the greatest place in the world'.

This book encompasses the three villages—if that is the right description—of Buckhurst Hill, Chigwell, and Loughton, which between 1933 and 1974 formed the Chigwell Urban District. This is a fascinating area of Essex, comprising as it does a large part of Epping Forest, suburban streets and shops, the meadows of the meandering river Roding, and good farmland. The three villages are situated on a series of hills which give fine views, particularly towards the south-west into London. These topographical features have shaped the history of the area, a history indeed to take pride in.

The three settlements began to take on the shape we know after the Norman Conquest; Chigwell and Loughton both appear in Domesday Book as small hamlets with a scattered population. Buckhurst Hill—the wooded hill covered with beeches— is first mentioned in 1135. Until 1894 Buckhurst Hill was part of the parish of Chigwell. Loughton's population lived around fairly isolated farmsteads including Alderton Hall and Debden House, and along the High Road, which led to Woodford in one direction but petered out into a forest track in the other; it was not until the 17th century that a through route to Epping was cut out of the woodland. The pattern of roads to serve the farms and fields had already been long established, and many of the streets and lanes we are familiar with today are undoubtedly at least a thousand years old.

Chigwell has grown only very slowly down the ages, and is today the most village-like of the three. Indeed, it can be said to comprise several hamlets, each with distinctive characteristics. Chigwell Village lies at the centre of a spider's web of narrow lanes which wind through open country; Chigwell Row lies to the south-east, clustered around the *Maypole* inn, with its historic associations with Dickens. There was once a popular mineral spring here, near what is now High View School. The Retreat restaurant looks modern, but it is in fact one of the oldest houses in Chigwell Row, with exposed 16th-century timbers within. Further along the Manor Road lies Grange Hill, which grew rapidly after the railway arrived in 1903, yet retains many fine views over a rural landscape. The postwar Grange Hill estate was taken out of Chigwell in 1965 and added to Redbridge, but historically Chigwell's boundary had included almost everything up to the New North Road. Finally, there is Chigwell Hatch, which merges with Woodford Bridge, with many newer houses gathered around the *Jolly Wheelers* and the three 'big houses'; Great West Hatch, Little West Hatch and the Manor House (now a convent).

Loughton's growth has largely been at the expense of the forest. Expansion towards the Roding was not possible over the marshy meadows, but there were gradual encroachments into the forest. It should be remembered that until recently, while it was recognised the forest trees were themselves a valuable resource, the open spaces and scrub which are a natural part of any forest were simply regarded as 'waste', which ought to be taken into cultivation. Landlords and villagers both saw fit to enclose and build upon forest 'waste', but the trickle of forest destruction threatened to turn into a flood in the 19th century, once royalty had lost interest in protecting the woodland as a hunting reserve. As the forest disappeared, local people defied landowners to practise their ancient right to lop wood, and the intelligentsia began to express alarm at the loss of the such a significant natural resource. A series of court cases was needed before Epping Forest was finally saved in 1878 for the enjoyment of everyone.

Hainault Forest, part of which lies within Chigwell, was not so fortunate. It was disafforested in 1851, and the destruction of the woodland commenced. Happily not all the trees disappeared; the intervention in 1903 of that great saviour of Epping Forest, Edward North Buxton, secured what remained of the tree cover, and Hainault Forest today is a country park open, like Epping Forest, for public enjoyment.

Loughton High Road was defined for centuries by the two historic inns at either end, the *Crown* and the *King's Head*. There were a few shops in between, and a cottage or two, but the bustling shopping centre we see today has only really come about since 1918. Much of Loughton High Road's architecture is indeed less than 30 years old.

While Loughton's growth was essentially infilling and expansion within an ancient village, Buckhurst Hill has been developed almost entirely out of forest and farm land. As with Loughton, the arrival of the railway in 1856 spurred development, but whereas in Loughton growth was quite slow, in Buckhurst Hill a thriving town sprang up around the station within twenty years. Buckhurst Hill was closest to London and was the first to achieve civic self-government; its small size meant there was—and remains—a strong community spirit.

Most of the grand houses built in the 17th and 18th centuries have now gone. These were country retreats for wealthy City merchants and courtiers, but the gradual urbanisation of the area has left few of them intact. Luxborough has gone, as has Rolls Park, though some smaller mansions such as Grange Court and Brook House (in Chigwell), North Farm, Beech House, Loughton Hall, and Alderton Hall (all in Loughton) survive. A second wave of grand Victorian edifices, built by nouveau riche industrialists and magnates, survives in better order. Holmehurst in Buckhurst Hill, Chigwell Hall, North Haven and Loughton Lodge are examples. Here too though there have been losses; Luctons in Buckhurst Hill, Brooklyn in Loughton. These houses required armies of domestic servants, which in turn attracted more people to the area.

The railways brought a tourist boom to the forest, and Loughton's streets rang to the shouts of happy Cockneys making their way to the forest. Tearooms sprang up everywhere to cater for the thirsty trippers, and at weekends hordes of cyclists poured out of London seeking the tranquillity and beauty which the forest offered. The tourist invasion was not universally welcomed; the visitors were condemned by some as insanitary and disruptive, and Loughton was long nicknamed 'Lousy Loughton' from the lice and fleas supposedly left behind by East Enders.

Chigwell remained largely untouched by these incursions, quietly focused as it had been for centuries around its architectural jewels of the parish church, Chigwell School and the *King's Head*, though as road transport improved increasing numbers of charabancs made their way out to the village to see the inn immortalised by Dickens. Chigwell however, remained under parish government, unlike Buckhurst Hill, which became an Urban District in 1894, and Loughton which followed suit in 1900. As mentioned earlier, the three combined in 1933 to form Chigwell Urban District. Forty years later, the winds of change swept through local government and a much larger local authority, Epping Forest District Council, was formed.

Change in the last few years has seemed bewilderingly rapid. The M11 has cut the area in half, driving its great tarmac swathe through the Roding Valley. Many much-loved family-run shops and businesses have disappeared, and there has been uncertainty and debate about the intensity of housing development. Though the area of the Forest has grown as more land has been purchased for it, there has been concern about the sheer pressure of numbers of those wishing to use it. Chigwell has become nationally famous through the television series *Birds of a Feather*, which has lampooned the ethics and lifestyle of the Londoner-made-good in Essex. Fortunately, both Essex Calf and Cockney Sparrer have a broad sense of humour which enables us to laugh at ourselves almost as loudly as we laugh at outsiders who think they know us.

Despite these concerns, much that is familiar and well-loved survives in Chigwell and Loughton and as the area faces new challenges and a new millennium, there seems every reason to suppose that the sense of neighbourliness, local pride and the feeling of belonging to a close-knit community will continue for many a long year.

Early History

The area has a very long history of settlement. Standing on a strategic spur of high ground in Epping Forest is Loughton Camp, a fortification probably built about 500 B.C. This period is known as the Iron Age; at that time Britain was divided into highly organised chiefdoms, with large-scale trade both inland and across to the Continent. Loughton Camp is roughly oval, defended by a single earth rampart enclosing about 12 acres. At one time, the camp must have commanded a spectacular view down the Roding valley, but by 1872 it was covered by dense undergrowth and entirely forgotten. In that year it was rediscovered by a Mr. B.H. Cowper, and excavations 10 years later found Iron-Age pottery within the ramparts. Camps like this were probably places of refuge and citadels rather than places to live.

Loughton Camp lies close to Ambresbury Banks, another Iron-Age fortification. It is now believed that these two forts were in separate—and presumably sometimes hostile—territories, roughly equivalent to the medieval hundreds of Ongar (Loughton Camp) and Waltham (Ambresbury Banks), so they may have acted as huge frontier posts, defining the boundary between the two areas.

In Chigwell, on land north-east of the Epping Forest Country Club, a Roman bath-house complex has been excavated, and coins, pottery, figurines and other material have been recovered in gravel-digging since at least 1790. This site is sometimes called 'Little London', and was probably the Roman town of *Durolitum*. This is known to have lain on one of the Roman roads between London and Chelmsford, though Romford has also claimed the title. The bathhouse was abandoned before A.D. 400, when determined robbers took the very stone from the walls, right down to the foundations. Roman rule ended at about this time, and the infrastructure which had previously provided the bathhouse with water, fuel for heating, and slaves to work the furnaces, collapsed quite suddenly.

In the fifth century, British warlords managed to maintain a semblance of Roman-style rule for a time, but Anglo-Saxon invaders quickly carved out new territories. One of these was the kingdom of Essex. In the Chigwell and Loughton area, it is likely that rural life carried on much as it had always done, although the forest may have expanded as the population declined through war and plague. It was in this Saxon period that the modern settlements of Chigwell and Loughton first began; both place-names are Old English, the language of the Anglo-Saxons, in origin. Chigwell seems to mean 'the spring of *Cicca*', while Loughton was 'the farm of *Luhha*', both *Cicca* and *Luhha* being Old English names. Woolston Hall lies so close to the Roman settlement site that it is possible that there was some continuity between the two, if only of the area farmed in the fertile Roding valley.

In 1062 Harold Godwineson (later King Harold II), re-founded Waltham Abbey and Edward the Confessor granted it various estates, which included *Tippedene* (Debden) and *Alwartune* (Alderton Hall, in Loughton). The bounds of these estates are given in the charter, but have never been analysed to assess their actual geographical extent. *Tippedene* means 'the valley of Tippa', but by the 13th century the original meaning had been forgotten and the estate was known as *Dupedene*, 'deep valley'.

Following the Norman invasion, Domesday Book, issued in 1087, gives two snapshots of life in the area, first as it was in 1066 under Edward the Confessor, and again in 1086 under William the Conqueror. Domesday assessed the taxable property of every estate in the land, so is an extremely useful guide to the population and its resources. Loughton was fragmented into eight separate estates. Five were held by Waltham Abbey itself, including one they had annexed from a free man. Other landowners were Robert Gernon, Peter of Valognes (who had displaced a free Anglo-Saxon named Wulfric), and the king himself. Chigwell comprised two estates, one held by Ralph of Livésy, and the other—Woolston Hall—held by the king. There were a total of 88 heads of households in both Chigwell and Loughton. The land must have been well-wooded as it was said to be capable of supporting 1,870 pigs, a notional measure of the size of forest but a very large number all the same. Seventy-six acres of meadows on the 10 estates of Chigwell and Loughton may well have consisted mainly of land beside the Roding, which was fertile but liable to seasonal flooding. Livestock comprised 28 cattle, 48 sheep, and 48 pigs, as well as 15 goats. There had been a water-mill at Chigwell in 1066, but this had been abandoned by 1086.

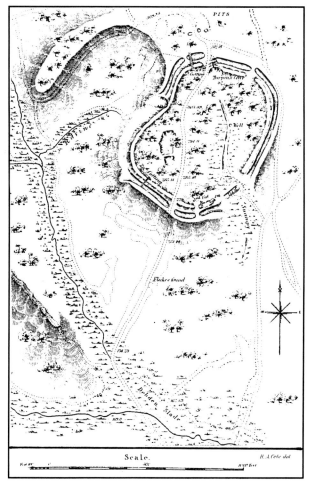

1 Loughton Camp, from an 1882 engraving. It was only recognised as an ancient fortification in 1872, by a Mr. B.H. Cowper, though as it lies in dense woodland this is perhaps not surprising. It may have been anciently known as *wud burh*, the fort in the wood, if this is the origin of the local name Woodbury, or it may be referred to in a charter of 1062 as *saeteres burh*, robbers' camp. The single earth rampart encloses 12 acres.

2 Roman burial urns and tableware pottery found during gravel extraction in Chigwell.

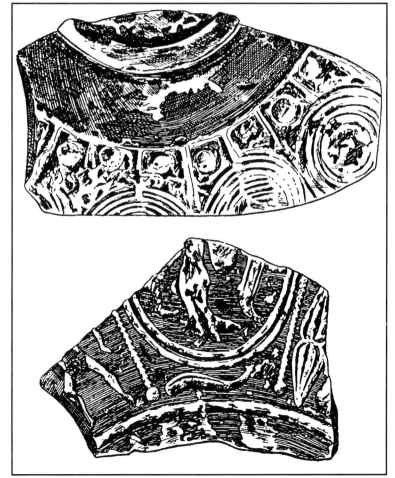

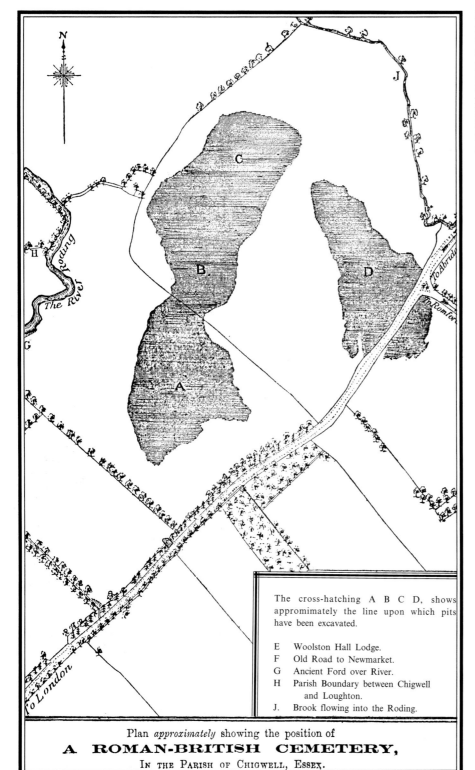

3 The Roman cemetery near Woolston Hall, Chigwell (from an archaeological survey of the 1870s). The presence of a cemetery near a main Roman road implies a fairly substantial settlement nearby; it has long been suggested that the site known as 'Little London' is the Roman town of *Durolitum*.

The cross-hatching A B C D, shows approximately the line upon which pits have been excavated.

E   Woolston Hall Lodge.
F   Old Road to Newmarket.
G   Ancient Ford over River.
H   Parish Boundary between Chigwell and Loughton.
J.   Brook flowing into the Roding.

Plan *approximately* showing the position of
A ROMAN-BRITISH CEMETERY,
In the Parish of Chigwell, Essex.

EĀDWEARD, 1062.

✠ IN nomine domini nostri Ihesu Christi, qui unus deus in trinitate ab omnibus se colentibus uencratur, et puro cordis affectu adoratur! Ego Eadwardus dei dono Anglorum rex in huius mundi decursu huius saeculi filiorum qui iusti inueniuntur studens exaltare cornu utpote regalis imperii iure rite roborati, accedant ad eum per callem iustitiae qui dat petentibus iuste et religiose uiuere. Haec tamen beata commutatio digne censetur in hoc saeculo ut cui foelicitas tantum deliberauerit animi quod mundialium grauedine cupiditatum postposita uelut granum frumenti a spinis suffocantibus aliquando uero dumetis arescentibus, decipiat in hunc tenorem emergi ut diuina uirtute firmatus uigeat suo creatori et domino. Istas etenim inter transitorias mundi procellas cuidam meorum comitum onomate Haroldo, quandam terram, quae antiquitus ab incolis illius loci nuncupatur Waltham, haereditario iure concessi, cum omnibus ad se pertinentibus, campis, pascuis, pratis, siluis, et aquis. Ex hinc sibi tantam deus suae pietatis gratiam contulit ut inter momentanea mundi desideria cogitaret foeliciter desudando coelestia; quinetiam ille qui omnia in omnibus operatur ut uult talem diuinae pietatis dulcedinem ut supramemoraui concessit ei, ut non solum dei cultor efficiatur, uerum etiam canonicae regulae strenuus institutor fieri credatur; nam haec diuinitus fidei declarationе et operum exhibitione caeterarumque aecclesiarum rerum plenitudine probauit euentus. Quis autem finis eius desiderii post haec euenerit, sapientia per Salomonem declarando prompsit, dum ait, 'Iustis dabitur desiderium bonum.' Enimuero rationali consilio ditatus ac suae non inmemor conditionis, in praescripto loco monasterium ad laudem domini nostri Ihesu Christi et sanctae crucis construxit. Primum concedens ei terram quae uocatur Norðlande, unde aecclesiam uillae antiquitus dotatam inuenit; post fundatum dehinc sacrae fidei monasterium ad normam sanctae dei aecclesiae dedicari fecit honorifice ob memoriam mei et coniugis meae nomine Eadiðae, patris ac matris, pro se suisque omnibus aiuis et defunctis sibi consanguinitate coniunctis. Hoc enim perplurimis, sanctorum, apostolorum, martyrum, confessorum, uirginum, reliquiis, ornauit. Hoc non solum terris, quarum uocabula post haec sunt recitanda, uerum etiam libris euangelicis, uestibus, ac diuersis ornamentorum generibus, templo domini congruentibus qui diuinis cultibus clare ac dulcedine imbutus attentius sanctae celebrationis templum excolere coepit ac uenerari. Quid plura? suae denique conditionis non immemor, ibidem quorundam cateruulam fratrum secundum auctoritatem sanctorum

hortatu excommunicamus et maledictione perpetua condempnamus omnes transgressores huius consularis donationis et regularis concessionis. Ðis synd ða landgemæra into Passefelde. Ðæt is, ærest of ðare ealdan hæcce æt freoðene felde into présta hlype; into ðam bece to Staun dúne; and of Staun dúne to Scealdeforda; and of Sceldeforda to coleboge welle; of ðére welle eft into ðære ealdan hæcce; and swá eft into freoðene felda. Ðis synd ða landgemæra into Welde. Ærest of Dellen norð into ðere gemýðe; eást into hafegæte; of hafegæte eást into ðam wulfpytte; of ðam pytte súð into ðam purce; of ðam purce súð to Freobearnes hlype; and swá into mannes laude; and ðanon eft into Dellen. Ðis synd ða landgemære into Upmynstre. Ærest at Tigelhyrste súð to ðare marcdíce; of ðare díce west in ingceburne; and of ðare burne norð into beccengáre; and of beccengáre norð andlang ðare stráte wald into stángáre; of stángáre norð into mannes lande; of mannes lande eft into Tigelhyrste. Ðis synd ða landgemære into Walbfare. Ærst of ðam æssce to ðære ældan hlype; of ðare hlype to ðare ealden wude hæcche; of ðære hæcce to ðare ealden stráte; and of ðare stráte to sandæcere; and of ðam æcere to beádewan eá; of ðare eá to wine bróce; of ðam bróce norð eft to ðan æssce. Ðis synd ða landgemære into Tippedene. Ærest in Tippaburne; of ðare burne úp to ðam héðe; and of ðam héðe to þecdene gemære wið æffan hecce; and swá into ðære eá; andlang ðære eá ðæt eft cymð in Tippeburne. Ðis synd ða landgemære into Ælwartone. Ærest æt Werdhæcce; of Werdhacce to eácrofte; of eácrofte into beolle póle; of ðam póle into Leófsiges mád; of Leófsiges mád into Omermád; of Omermád into Æðeríces hlype; of ðare hlype into wulfhlype; of wulfhlype into þesfalde; of þesfalde into stánweges hacce; of stánweges hacce into Sateres byrig. Ðis synd ða landgemære into Wudeforde. Ærest in Angríces burne to ealdermannes hæcce to ðær cynges hæcce; of ðær cynges hæcce eft into Angríces burne. Ðis synd ða landgemære into Lámbehyðe. Ærest æt brixges stáne; and swá ford þurwh ðane gráf to ðam mærcdíce; and swá to bulce treó; and fram bulce treó to hyse; and fram hyse to Ælsyges hæcce; and swá ést to ðare stráte; and swá andlang stréte ést to brixes stán. Ðis synd ða landgemære into Nassingan. Ðat is, hárst of cerlen hacce andlang mearce to scelden mǽre; and of scelden mére to ðare burnan; and of ðáre burnan to buterwyelle; and of buterwelle to Ðuroldes gemáren; and of Ðuroldes gemáren eft andlang marce to cerlen hacce; and seó mæd ðe ðárto

---

4   The opening passage of the charter of 1062, *above left*, in which Edward the Confessor grants land to Waltham Abbey as part of its re-foundation by the ill-fated Harold Godwineson.

5   Part of the 1062 charter, *above right*, which lists the boundaries, in Old English, of the estates of Debden and Alderton Hall.

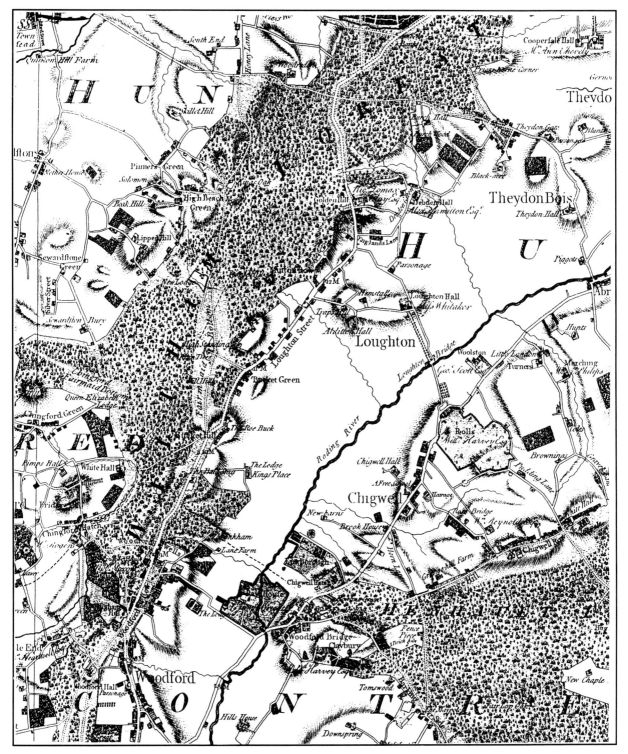

6 Part of Chapman & André's map of Essex, 1777, showing Chigwell and Loughton. Bucket Hill and Bucket Green are the present-day Buckhurst Hill. Loughton consists mainly of one long street with Epping Forest to the west and a few farmsteads—Alditton Hall (Alderton Hall) and Loughton Hall—to the east. Chigwell School can be seen, as can the great estates of Luxborough and Rolls Park. Much of the street pattern is as it is today, and as it had been for many centuries. The shape of Chigwell and Loughton seen in this map is therefore probably not very similar to what it had been for several centuries.

Churches

The district's two ancient parish churches, St Mary's Chigwell and St Nicholas Loughton, both still stand, though only St Mary's is still in use as a parish church.

St Mary's Chigwell had Norman origins, and has a fine Norman doorway on the south side. However, the church was more than doubled in size in 1886; in this rebuilding, the ancient nave became the south aisle, and a new nave was built to the north. The timber belfry is 15th century. One of its chief glories is a fine brass of Samuel Harsnett, founder of Chigwell School. Chigwell Row became a separate ecclesiastical parish in 1860, and All Saints was built seven years later. This church was once rather condescendingly described by Norman Scarfe in the *Shell Guide to Essex* as 'excellent— *of its sort*'.

Loughton's original parish church, St Nicholas, stood close to Loughton Hall, and was a humble building with a timber belfry. It was entirely rebuilt in 1877, but by then it had become little more than the private chapel of the Maitland family, lords of the manor of Loughton. Indeed a new church, St John's, had been built nearer the village in 1846, in what is now Church Lane. Sydney Smirke was the architect. Loughton continued to grow, and a further church, St Mary's, was built in the High Road in 1871. Buckhurst Hill, originally part of Chigwell, became a separate ecclesiastical parish in 1838; its church of St John the Baptist was built in 1837.

Like other parts of Essex, Chigwell and Loughton had a strong tradition of non-conformity, and the area is liberally supplied with chapels and meeting halls of varying Protestant traditions. Congregationalists were active in Chigwell from 1804, and Baptists in Loughton from 1813. After a brief false start in Chigwell in 1827, Methodism came late to the area, surprising in an area so well trodden by Wesley. An iron church was put up in 1880 in Buckhurst Hill, while after a short period based in Forest Road, Loughton, a new church was established 1903, in High Road opposite Traps Hill. Many older residents will recall this redbrick Gothic-style church, replaced in recent years with a strikingly modern building which is quite a Loughton landmark. Not forgetting Roman Catholicism, represented by the church of St Edmund of Canterbury in Traps Hill, which is also an arresting example of modern church architecture. It was built in 1958 following a disastrous fire in an earlier building.

7 St Mary's, Chigwell. The engraving is from Elizabeth Ogborne's *History of Essex*, published in 1812.

8 The Norman south doorway of St Mary's, Chigwell, dating from about 1180.

9 St Nicholas' Church, Loughton. This original church was rebuilt in 1877. The churchyard contains the tombs of two worthy ladies: Elizabeth French, the founder of the construction firm French, and Sarah Martin, who wrote *Old Mother Hubbard*.

10 A postcard view of St Mary's, Loughton.

11 St John's, Buckhurst Hill, *c.*1868. This shows the church in its original form, with the added chancel of 1864-5. As the population has grown, the church has been enlarged several times, notably with the addition of a large south aisle, and a new tower and spire. On the right is the schoolroom, built in 1839, together with the additional schoolroom added in 1866-7. This now forms part of St John's (C.ofE.) Primary School.

12 All Saints' Church, Chigwell Row. The massive tower on its hilltop site can be seen for miles around.

13 The imposing Congregational Church in Palmerston Road, Buckhurst Hill. The main body of the church has recently been demolished and redeveloped as retirement flats; only the tower survives.

14 Loughton Union Church. Built in 1860-1, this Italianate building replaced an earlier chapel of 1813. The church is shared by Baptists and the United Reformed Church.

15   King's Place Church, Buckhurst Hill. Built in 1887 for a dissident Congregational faction, the church was sold in 1909 to the Baptists. It was demolished in the 1960s and replaced with a modern church.

16   Alfred Road Mission in Buckhurst Hill. Built as a Congregational mission hall in 1863, it was rebuilt *c*.1925, when this photograph was taken, by Charles Linder, a prominent Buckhurst Hill philanthropist. It was used by the Salvation Army from about 1936. The building survives but is no longer a church.

Forest

Epping Forest, that seemingly timeless swathe of woodland, is much less than 2,000 years old. At its heart are two Iron-Age fortifications, Loughton Camp and Ambresbury Banks. Such camps were invariably built—probably as defensive retreats—on high ground with clear views around. So when they were constructed, the forest could not have existed to anything like its present extent. Surprisingly enough, it is also fairly certain that Roman Britain had less woodland than today. It was probably during the Anglo-Saxon period that the great forest we know today arose. By the time of the Norman Conquest, the forest had become attractive as a place for hunting, and it was the Norman kings who enacted a series of laws which created the royal Forests of England. The distinction between Forest and forest—maintained in this book—is an important one. Forest meant the land covered by Forest laws, while forest is nowadays simply a synonym for woodland. So, although the Forest of Essex, probably created by Henry I, covered almost the whole county, it was not the case, as was once believed, that there was unbroken woodland from London to Colchester. Forest Law had its own courts and officials and penalties for infringement could be severe. However, there were benefits to living within Forest bounds, including the right to graze cattle on open—'waste'—land, and the right to take, or 'lop' timber, which could be used for winter fuel. The monarch did not own the Forest, which remained private land, merely the right to keep deer in it, and to maintain the Forest courts.

The Forest of Essex eventually fragmented into several components, one of which in south-west Essex became known as Waltham Forest, later Epping Forest. Charles I's attempts to revive the ancient Forest Laws as a means of extracting money from landowners was a significant factor in his eventual downfall. By this time, there was little royal interest in deer-hunting, the original reason for establishing forest; the last monarchs who enjoyed the chase in Epping were Henry VIII, Elizabeth I and James I. As Forest Law fell into disuse, landowners enclosed more and more land for agriculture and building, and prosecuted villagers for exercising their ancient rights. Matters reached a head in 1871 when the City of London's Corporation prosecuted landowners for illegal enclosures. The Epping Forest Act of 1878 was the result, and the forest was dedicated 'to the use and enjoyment of my people for all time' by Queen Victoria when she visited High Beach in 1882.

17   The Pulpit Oak, in Lord's Bushes, Buckhurst Hill, *c.*1889. Without the protection of the Epping Forest Act in 1878, Lord's Bushes would undoubtedly have disappeared under the housing estates which were already beginning to surround it. Fortunately, the Act stipulated that all land open and unenclosed in 1851 had to remain open or be returned to the forest where it had since been enclosed or built over. This saved the 90 acres of Lord's Bushes and several other fragments of woodland in the area.

18   Golding's Hill Pond, Loughton, *c.*1875. This scenic spot has been a popular picnic site for over a century.

19   Lopping Hall, Loughton; the Station Road front, *c.*1933. The Epping Forest Act extinguished the villagers' rights to lop wood from the forest, a right they had tenaciously defended against local landowners. In compensation for the loss of these ancient privileges, the City of London paid £7,000, and with this money, Lopping Hall was built as a social facility for the people of Loughton.

20 The Warren, *c.*1900. The residence of the Superintendent of the Forest. It began life in the 18th century as *The Reindeer*, a rural resort for wealthy patrons. In about 1800 it became the home of General Grosvenor, a friend of Wellington's.

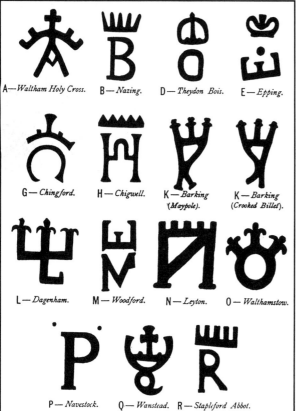

A—*Waltham Holy Cross.*   B—*Nazing.*   D—*Theydon Bois.*   E—*Epping.*

G—*Chingford.*   H—*Chigwell.*   K—*Barking (Maypole).*   K—*Barking (Crooked Billet).*

L—*Dagenham.*   M—*Woodford.*   N—*Leyton.*   O—*Walthamstow.*

P—*Navestock.*   Q—*Wanstead.*   R—*Stapleford Abbot.*

21 Forest cattle marks. Cattle and horses are permitted to graze anywhere within the Forest, provided they belong to residents (known as Commoners) owning at least half an acre of open Forest land in a parish within the Forest. To prevent misuse of this ancient privilege, each beast has to be branded with a mark indicating its parish of origin.

22 Staples Road Reservoir, Loughton. Long since filled in, the pond stood on the edge of the forest where Loughton Brook crosses Staples Road, and was a popular resort for children visiting the Shaftesbury Retreat nearby. Indeed, the children's presence was one of the reasons for creating the reservoir as the Shaftesbury Retreat placed a large extra demand on the town's water supply.

Drawn on Stone by. C.M.H. 1827

Shooters Hill *From Chigwell Row.*

23 Grange Hill, Chigwell, from an 1842 watercolour by J. Cawthorn. Although Grange Hill did not form part of either Epping or Hainault Forest, its well-wooded character of olden days can be clearly seen in this picture. The Grange Hill estate now covers these hills; built up by the London County Council, until 1965 it lay within Chigwell, but was then moved into the London Borough of Redbridge.

24 Shooters Hill from Chigwell Row; an engraving from 1827. There is still a good view of Shooters Hill (Kent) from many parts of Chigwell and Loughton, though the land in between is now almost entirely built up. On a clear day, the eye can see as far as the North Downs and Crystal Palace.

Houses

The arrival of the railway in 1856 gave some impetus to the development of Buckhurst Hill and Loughton, but the area remained surprisingly rural until well into the 20th century. Large-scale development did not take place because no cheap workmen's fares into London were available, and the Forest was inviolate.

However, the area was attractive to London merchants and business-people from the 17th century onwards as it combined the advantages of a country retreat with easy access to London; Loughton is less than twelve miles from Charing Cross. However even now, this is not suburbia; the stout fences and high holly hedges of many houses recall a time not so long ago when it was necessary to keep out straying cattle and deer.

In Wright's *History of Essex*, published in 1835, Loughton is described as 'distinguished by its numerous genteel houses and beautiful and picturesque scenery', while over a century later Chigwell was described by Marcus Crouch in his *Essex* (Batsford Counties of England series) thus; 'Chigwell ... has retained miraculously its village centre and much of its village spirit. Few [places] are so satisfying as the group of buildings around the church and inn at Chigwell'.

This chapter provides an opportunity to see some of the houses lost through demolition and neglect. Many fine mansions have disappeared as the villages developed. However, even the most built-up parts of the district can be architecturally interesting. The sheer diversity of house styles is astonishing, and in many roads (take for instance, at random, Queens Road in Loughton), there are scarcely two houses alike. In part this is due to the very slow build-up of the area, with development spread over a long period of time.

The area has a reputation for 'a high class of property' as the *Official Guide* for 1950 described it; Chigwell in particular is associated with large modern houses set in more or less substantial grounds, some built in striking and individual styles. A walk along Hainault Road and Manor Road will confirm this, and Loughton too has some very fine large houses in Alderton Hill, Spareleaze Hill, Tycehurst Hill and elsewhere.

Humbler dwellings are represented here too. There is little natural building stone in Essex, and for centuries houses were built out of timber. Many weatherboarded houses survive in the area, especially near the forest. In the 19th century, neat brick-built terraces were erected, particularly in Buckhurst Hill, to house railway workers and other artisans, and these are also featured here, as are the semi-detached homes built between the wars, suburban dream homes for many a young couple.

25 The east front of Luxborough House. This spectacular mansion was built in 1716-20 for Robert Knight, Baron Luxborough. He was cashier of the South Sea Company and after being ruined in the South Sea Bubble he fled abroad. However, he made a remarkable comeback, receiving a royal pardon and ennoblement. The building was demolished in 1800.

26 The south front of Luxborough House. Luxborough Lane leads to the site of the house.

27 Rolls Park, Chigwell. The manor was earlier known as Barringtons, and was built up by Sir Eliab Harvey, nephew of William Harvey who discovered the circulation of blood. A famous descendant of his was his namesake Admiral Sir Eliab Harvey (1758-1830), commander of the *Téméraire* at the Battle of Trafalgar. The building, demolished in the 1950s, originated in the 17th century, with additions in the 18th century.

28 Luctons in Buckhurst Hill, *c*.1900, was the home of the Powell family. Luctons Avenue is named after this fine house, which was demolished in 1910. Built in the 16th century, it was also said to have had associations with Dick Turpin. Here in 1900 the Powells held a very special celebration of the Relief of Mafeking, as Baden-Powell was a distant relation.

29 Knighton, in Buckhurst Hill, showing the rear elevation and croquet lawn. This was the home of Edward North Buxton, who helped save Epping Forest from destruction. It was demolished in 1935 to make way for the Knighton estate.

30 Monkham's Farm, Monkham Lane, Buckhurst Hill. Though this farm is more usually associated with Woodford, where much of its estate lay, it was actually situated just within Buckhurst Hill. This view shows the south front on 2 December 1935, shortly before demolition to make way for the Monkhams estate.

31 Hawstead, a substantial Victorian house in Buckhurst Hill, situated where the modern cul-de-sac Hawstead now lies. Hawstead was adjacent to Ardmore (hence Ardmore Lane), another very large Victorian mansion which was once owned by Dr. Barnardo.

32 No. 97 Albert Road (Herbert Cottages), Buckhurst Hill. The photograph was taken c.1905. This cottage is typical of the many built in the late 19th century in Lower Buckhurst Hill. Note the queen conches on the window ledge. Were they souvenirs from some seafaring expedition, or perhaps simply prizes at a local fair?

33 A postcard view of Chigwell Hall. The manor and estate of Chigwell Hall has a complex history. The original manor house stood beside the Roding, beneath what is now the Roding Valley nature reserve, but this had been abandoned by the 17th century. A new manor house was built in Roding Lane, at the property now known as Bramstons, which was itself rebuilt c.1870. The house which then became known as Chigwell Hall is now the Metropolitan Police Sports Club. This was built in 1876, having been designed on a grand scale by the architect Norman Shaw. Confusingly enough, there is also a building known as Chigwell Manor House, now a convent, at Chigwell Hatch.

34 Grange Court, Chigwell, from a sale catalogue of 1924. A spectacular 17th-century building, largely rebuilt in 1774. It was purchased by Chigwell School in 1946 as a memorial to those pupils and old boys killed in the Second World War, and now forms part of the school.

35 Brook House, Chigwell. Another very fine building, with 15th-century origins, it stands in the High Road. The present building dates largely from the 18th century.

36 Turnours Hall, Gravel Lane, *left*. A substantial and surviving farmhouse on the rural fringes of Chigwell. Like Brook House, this building was already in existence by the 15th century.

37 Woolston Hall, Chigwell, *below left*, from a watercolour by John Cawthorn, 1825. This manor was recorded in Domesday Book, at which time it was directly owned by William the Conqueror. The estate was held by a single family, the Scotts, for almost three centuries from 1485-1780. It was sold in 1939 to the Co-operative Wholesale Society, who turned it into a sports club; it is now privately run, and known as Epping Forest Country Club. The oldest part of the building is 15th century, with timber-framing, plaster and brick, with many subsequent additions.

38 The Manor House, Chigwell, *below*. Standing in High Road, Chigwell Hatch, this fine building, now a convent of the Sisters of the Sacred Hearts of Jesus and Mary, occupies a commanding position. The house, which was for a short time in the late 18th century Chigwell's manor house, is Georgian, though with later additions. This photograph, *c*.1882, shows the garden front.

39 Harsnetts, a charming 17th-century building facing Chigwell School.

40 John Elsee's fine Georgian house at Chigwell Row. The oldest surviving building in Chigwell Row is the Retreat, now a restaurant and extensively rebuilt, but incorporating parts of a 16th-century house; the exposed timbers can still be seen inside the bar. One of the finest surviving old houses in Chigwell Row is Hainault House, recently restored, which stands near the *Maypole*.

41 Great West Hatch, *c*.1953. A hospital for over a century, Great West Hatch began life as a Georgian house *c*.1800, built of yellow stock brick. The hospital is scheduled for closure (1995) and the future of the building is uncertain.

42 Little West Hatch. Facing Great West Hatch on the other side of Luxborough Lane is Little West Hatch, a fine building which remains a private residence. The photograph dates from *c*.1890.

43 Forest Lane, Chigwell, *above*. A pleasant scene of suburban semis, all built between the wars. Note the rural-sounding name 'The Brambles' on the nearest gate.

44 Loughton Hall in 1899, *above right*. This Domesday manor has a fascinating history. Mary Tudor was its owner two months before she became queen in 1553. In 1578 it passed to the Wroth family, who were prominent in public and court life; they held it until 1738. In the 19th century, the Maitland family held the manor, and dominated parish life. As major landowners, they were bound up with the controversy over the future of the Forest. In 1944 the house and estate were sold to the London County Council. The Debden estate was built on the land, and the house given over to community use.

45 The original Loughton Hall, *c.1821, right*. This burnt down in a spectacular fire in 1836, to be replaced by the present building, which the Rev. J.W. Maitland had built in 1878. The original Hall, visited by James I, Queen Anne, Ben Johnson and Sir Philip Sidney, was mainly 16th century.

46 North Farm, *left*, was earlier known as Dennison's farm. This view shows the yard in 1905. The name was taken from one John North, who occupied the farm in 1717, and it was the last working farm in Loughton. A great swathe of the open land around it is now (1995) being transformed into a housing estate known as Great Woodcotes.

47 Old cottages in The Hole, Loughton, April 1928, *below left*. These cottages, off Woodbury Hill had been condemned by the District Council as insanitary and were scheduled for demolition when this photograph was taken. However, the order was reprieved and the cottages refurbished.

48 Suburbia in Loughton, *below*. Queen's Park (later Queens) Road was built up over a long period, between 1886 and 1939. There are fine views over Loughton and beyond from the houses at the top of the road.

49 A minute weatherboarded cottage in York Hill. It was demolished in the 1920s.

50 Whitaker Almshouses, Loughton, 1928, with Mrs. Blissett seated in the porch. These almshouses, overlooking Arewater Green, were built in 1827 through the generosity of the Whitaker family, lords of the manor until 1825.

51   Church House, Church Lane, Loughton, on 29 August 1896. At this time Church Lane only led into fields and was known as Blind Lane.

52 Alderton Hall, in Alderton Hill, is one of the three Domesday manors of Loughton, and is a weatherboarded building dating from the 16th century with later additions. It has a chequered history, and in recent years has been particularly associated with the actor Jack Watling, a colourful local character who lived there from 1954-1981.

53 Brooklyn, Traps Hill, *c*.1900. This massive pile was built for the Loughton cornmerchant George Gould in 1888, and was demolished in 1967 to make way for Loughton Library. The shopping parade on the High Road in front of the site was named Brooklyn Parade after the house, as was Brooklyn Avenue.

54 Forest Villa (earlier The Retreat), Staples Road, Loughton was built in 1882. This was the house of Robert Hunter, a remarkable 19th-century polymath. His interests encompassed languages, Indian history and religion, lexicography, Christianity, astronomy and palaeontology. From his geological studies, he was an early adherent of evolution. He was a fiery nonconformist minister in a Docklands chapel, but freely opened his large house to parties of poor East End children to enable them to benefit from a day in the forest. There is a splendid view from the belvedere or lantern, where Hunter had his own astronomical observatory. The house still stands.

55 Ree House, Englands Lane, seen here in 1904. The house, once a nonconformist chapel, was demolished in 1906.

56 Traps Hill House, Loughton. This striking building, which stands at the summit of Traps Hill, has a 16th-century core but was extensively remodelled in the early 19th century. It was the subject of much controversy in the 1970s when permission to demolish the house and redevelop the site was refused.

Industry

Agriculture and forestry were the most important local trades until well into the 20th century. There were other industries, but these were on a smaller scale. As the place-names Tile-Kiln Farm and Potters Close testify, there were brick-, tile- and pottery-manufacturing sites in the area from the 15th century onwards. In Loughton, these were located on Goldings Hill, Englands Lane, Nursery Road, between Albion Hill and Warren Hill, and York Hill. In Chigwell, Sir Eliab Harvey was operating a brickworks near Rolls Park in the 17th century, and there was a further works at Luxborough. In Buckhurst Hill, a brickworks was opened in the 1860s by Mrs. Elizabeth French; the company she founded grew to become an international construction corporation. The number of large houses in the area meant that there was a constant demand for domestic servants too. Nursery gardens are scattered throughout the area, the oldest being Fairhead's in Nursery Road, first established as Paul's in 1862.

A number of small industries also flourished, including watchmaking. Prominent local watchmakers included John Roger Arnold (*fl*.1800-43) of Marchings in Gravel Lane, Thomas Prest (d.1852) and his son, also Thomas (d.1877), both of Chigwell Row, and Alfred Attfield Osborne (1864-1946) of Buckhurst Hill.

Since the building of the Debden estate, light industrial units have been established beside the Roding at Oakwood Hill and Langston Road, on the site of the prefab bungalows, built to house those made homeless by the Blitz. This is also the site for the Bank of England Printing Works, the largest employer in Debden.

57   A rural scene on Traps Hill at the turn of the century. A hay elevator is stacking the crop while men and horses rest briefly.

58 The malt-house, North Farm, 1908. This was the last working farm in Loughton. Malt-houses were common in many Essex farms, and all kinds of preserving, pickling, brewing and distilling were carried out in them.

59 Albion Granaries, *c*.1903. These granaries were Loughton's largest, and occupied a prominent site in the High Road, where Safeway supermarket (earlier Presto) now stands. The demolition of the granary in 1981—by which time the building had been used for some years by Brown's Engineering—caused much local controversy. The clock from the granary (seen at top right) was incorporated into the new supermarket façade.

G. GOULD & SONS

ALBION GRANARIES, LOUGHTON.

AGRICULTURAL, VEGETABLE, AND FLOWER SEEDS.

IMPORTERS OF DUTCH & OTHER FLOWER ROOTS

Catalogue forwarded on application, post free.

CORN, HAY, STRAW & FLOUR MERCHANTS.
Furniture Removed to all Parts.
G. GOULD & SONS,
LOUGHTON, ESSEX.
Albion Granaries

Our Warehousing Rooms are some of the Driest, and most substantially built in Essex.

60 An 1893 advertisement for Albion Granaries.

T. ARCHER,

Corn, Flour, and Seed Merchant,

BUCKHURST HILL.

Price Lists and Seed Catalogues Free on Application.

Scotch Oatmeals Direct from the Mills.
Beans and Peas, Lentils, Rice, Tapioca, &c., &c.

GOODS WAREHOUSED.
T. ARCHER,
BUCKHURST HILL.
Furniture Removed by Road or Rail.
ESTIMATES FREE.

EXPERIENCED MEN ONLY EMPLOYED.

Large, Dry, and Well-Ventilated Rooms for Warehousing.

61 An 1896 advertisement for Archer's, corn-merchants of Buckhurst Hill.

Mrs. E. ASKEW,

CARTER AND CONTRACTOR,

FOREST ROAD & SMART'S LANE,

LOUGHTON.

LICENSED PROPRIETRESS OF HORSES And WAGGONETTES.

Dealer in Faggots, Pea Sticks, &c.

WILLIAM LEBBON,

Practical Boot, Shoe and Slipper Manufacturer,

QUEEN'S PARK CORNER, YORK HILL,

LOUGHTON.

All kinds of Cripples' Boots (Cork or otherwise) made on the most approved principles.

Hunting, Shooting, Fishing, Cricketing and Walking Boots and Shoes made to Order.

Materials and Workmanship Guaranteed of the Highest Quality.

A well-selected Stock of ready-made Goods always on hand.

Families waited on at their own Residences.

REPAIRS NEATLY EXECUTED.

62 An 1893 advertisement for Loughton trades; the Askew family were prominent jobbing contractors and hauliers in both Buckhurst Hill and Loughton.

W. ARNILL,

Veterinary Shoeing Forge

Horses Shod on the Latest Science. **LOUGHTON, ESSEX.**

SMITHS WORK IN GENERAL.

63 A trade card for Arnill's forge, situated on Church Hill, Loughton. The forge, demolished in 1995, was until recently occupied by the Domextra water-softener works. There had been a forge here since at least as far back as 1711; William Arnill was occupying it by 1876.

64 As the town expanded, house-builders and road-builders enjoyed a steady trade in Loughton. Here a new road is being made from York Hill up to Loughton Lodge. The date is October 1905, and the road is now known as Steeds Way.

Inns and Public Houses

Loughton in particular seems to have more than its fair share of pubs. A brisk walk down the High Road reveals the *Crown*, the *Royal Standard*, the *Holly Bush*, the *Last Post* (Loughton's newest opened in 1994), the *King's Head*, with the *Wheatsheaf* next door, and the *Prince of Wales* along Church Hill, while Forest Road and Smart's Lane boast the *Royal Oak*, the *Carpenters' Arms* and the *Victoria Tavern*. Along Epping New Road are the *Reindeer*, the *Warren Wood*, *Robin Hood*, and further up, the *Wake Arms*. On the other side of Loughton the *Mother Hubbard* commemorates Loughton resident Sarah Martin (1768-1826). Buckhurst Hill has the *Roebuck*, the *Bald Faced Stag*, the *Queens*, the *Railway Tavern*, the *Prince of Wales*, the *Three Colts* and *Monkhams*, amongst others, while across the Roding in Chigwell, the *King's Head* was immortalised by Charles Dickens as the *Maypole* in *Barnaby Rudge*; other pubs in Chigwell include the *King William IV*, the *Maypole* and the nearby *Two Brewers* and the *Retreat*, not forgetting the *Bald Hind* and the *Jolly Wheelers*.

Many of these tavern names can clearly be associated with the Forest, and date from the latter half of the 19th century when the Forest was opening up to visitors and trippers. No doubt the local industries (agriculture, brick- and tile-making) were thirsty work too. Some of these public houses began life as tearooms and evolved, though virtually all of them maintained tearooms to cater for what was then a large temperance movement, as well as family parties in search of light refreshment. However, some of the inns are of considerable antiquity, notably Chigwell's *King's Head*, and also the *Maypole*. The *Maypole* is just one of the many older inns which have been rebuilt, sometimes several times, including Buckhurst Hill's *Roebuck* and *Bald Faced Stag*, and Loughton's *King's Head* and *Crown*.

Rebuilding, renovation and modernisation have always been part of the life of public houses. However, recently there has been a sad trend on the part of a few landlords for renaming local inns, and several historic hostelries have (temporarily, no doubt) received whimsical names more redolent of the American Mid-West than rural Essex. So, the *Reindeer* must now be styled the *Colorado Exchange*, while the wholly appropriate *Bald Faced Stag* has recently, despite protests received the soubriquet of *Jeffersons*. Also in Buckhurst Hill, the *Prince of Wales* is now *B52s*, while on the road to Epping the rebuilt *Wake Arms* has become *City Limits*. Most lamentable of all has been the metamorphosis of the historic *Crown* into the meaningless *Rat and Carrot*, in the teeth of local opposition.

65 The *King's Head*, Chigwell. Dickens described this hostelry as, 'an old building with more gable ends than a lazy man would care to count on a sunny day'. It dates from the early 16th century, but there have been many later additions. The *King's Head* was immortalised in Dickens' *Barnaby Rudge*, where it appears as the *Maypole*. Tudor timbering has been exposed on the façade in recent years, but the concrete balls, still painted white, remain as shown in this picture.

66 Inside the *King's Head*, Chigwell, showing a postcard view of 'The Old Chester Room' (misspelt on the postcard). With its fine 17th-century panelling, this room originally served as the venue for the Forest's Court of Attachments (one of the lesser courts, set up to resolve minor infringements and disputes). Since those days it has been used for many years as a restaurant.

67 The old gatehouse beside the *King's Head*, Chigwell. Rather dubiously claimed to date from the 14th century, this curious building contained a jury box and prison cell, having at one time been associated with the Forest Court of Attachments. Its demolition in 1929 was described at the time as 'ruthless ... vandalism ... a lasting disgrace to the owners'.

68 The *Bald Faced Stag*, Buckhurst Hill. This inn was first recorded in 1725, but is probably considerably older than that. An important staging post, the *Stag* was the site of a grisly hanging in 1752; John Swan and Elizabeth Jeffrey were executed for shooting Elizabeth Jeffrey's uncle, Joseph Jeffreys in Walthamstow.

69 The *Crown*, Loughton. This splendid photograph shows an outing of four-in-hand coaches, date unknown, in front of the redbrick inn. It was from this inn that old Thomas Willingale set out on 12 November 1860 to exercise the ancient right of lopping wood from the forest. The lord of the manor had thrown a banquet at the *Crown* (in other accounts, the *King's Head*) in an attempt to distract the loppers, but old Tom was not to be confounded. After cutting some timber, he returned to the inn triumphantly bearing the bough aloft to prove that their rights had not been thwarted. The building was demolished in the 1960s, and a parade of shops erected which incorporated a smaller pub.

"Crown" Hotel, LOUGHTON.

Proprietor - - - GEORGE WILLIS.

Large Hall in Grounds adjoining for Banquets, Concerts, Garden Parties, etc.

LARGEST BILLIARD ROOM IN ESSEX.

Special Old Blended Scotch Whiskey delivered to any address, 20s. per gallon.

LIVERY AND BAIT STABLES, GOOD LOOSE BOXES, AND EVERY ACCOMMODATION FOR HUNTERS.

70 This 1896 advertisement for the *Crown* makes a stirring claim; 'the largest billiard room in Essex'! Intending patrons might note that, a century later, whisky is no longer 20s. a gallon.

71 The *Roebuck*, Buckhurst Hill, in 1890. Shortly after this photograph was taken, the *Roebuck* was rebuilt on a grand scale, with only a small part of this building, just the first gable on the left, incorporated into the new structure. It is now a Forte hotel.

72 Little has changed since this photograph of the *Foresters' Arms* was taken a century ago. Standing at the top of Baldwin's Hill, the *Foresters'* commands extensive views over Epping Forest. The Tea Gardens, once a ubiquitous adjunct to pubs in the area, have now disappeared, and a small extension has been added on the opposite side, but the main front survives virtually unaltered. The building dates back to 1865, when the land it stands on was first enclosed from the Forest.

73 The *Gardeners' Arms*, at the top of Loughton's York Hill, in April 1899, photographed from Woodbury Hill. From this point, known locally as Grout's Corner, there is one of the most extensive views in the south-west of the county, looking across Metropolitan Essex to London and the hills of Kent. The *Gardeners' Arms* began life as a tearoom. Next door, the ancient timbered Brittons Cottages still stand, and bear the date 1525.

74 The *King William IV*, Chigwell High Road, in 1936. The pub was rebuilt in 1983 a short distance from this original building, in traditional Essex weatherboarding. The original inn now serves as an estate agents.

75 The old *Maypole*, Chigwell Row, from a painting. Although Dickens used the *King's Head* for his Chigwell setting in *Barnaby Rudge*, he changed its name to the *Maypole*, based on this Chigwell Row inn. He explained this blending of the two inns thus, 'the truth is, I patched it. The place in my mind was Chigwell Row, but I moved the *King's Head Inn*, to the site of the real *Maypole*, as more suitable for my story'. This inn was eventually replaced by a new inn directly in the Lambourne Road; the original inn was for many years divided into two tenements before its demolition.

76 The *Winston Churchill* is one of the newer public houses in the area. Occupying a prominent position on the corner of Debden Broadway and Rectory Lane, the name commemorates local associations with Churchill, who was MP for the Epping constituency (which included Chigwell and Loughton) from 1924-45.

77 Loughton's *Holly Bush* is seen here decorated for Queen Victoria's 1897 diamond jubilee. The inn stands, largely unaltered, almost opposite the *Crown*. Both the *Holly Bush* and the nearby *Royal Standard* stand on land enclosed from the Forest in 1844.

78 A very early photograph of the *King's Head*, Loughton. King's Green can be seen in front of the inn—now the site for Loughton's war memorial, this was earlier known as Cage Green as the village lock-up used to be located there. This is the second *King's Head*, a substantial building which replaced an earlier wooden building further up York Hill, and itself replaced this century by a still larger building.

79 The *Robin Hood*, on Epping New Road, dates back to *c*.1865. It was immensely popular in the late 19th and early 20th centuries, as it was a destination, meeting place, and picnic spot for many visitors to the Forest. In this postcard view, a thirsty horse takes a drink from a trough while on the other side of the road is what appears to be a photographer, with his camera on a tripod and other equipment nearby.

80 A postcard of the *Prince of Wales*, in Lower Queen's Road, Buckhurst Hill, *above*. As usual, there is a tearoom annexe.

81 Chigwell also boasts a *Prince of Wales*, in Manor Road, *above left*. This rustic-looking inn had simple wooden benches with sawn-off tree trunks for tables placed outside, while to the left, a separate door led into a tearoom.

THE JOLLY WHEELERS, CHIGWELL.

82 The *Jolly Wheelers* in Chigwell Hatch, *left*, towards Woodford Bridge. The man with the wheelbarrow looks busy but it is not clear what he is doing. On the right, a poster advertises an appearance by Kate Carney at the 'Empire' music-hall.

People

Buckhurst Hill, Chigwell and Loughton have been home to many famous men and women down the ages. The beauty of the forest has long attracted artists and writers. The sculptor Jacob Epstein lived at a house on Baldwins Hill from 1931-50. Kipling, when a boy, stayed at Golding's Hill Farm. W.W. Jacobs (1863-1943), best known for his humorous short stories, also lived on Golding's Hill. His sister Helen Mary Jacobs (1888-1970) was an accomplished book illustrator. Many of the tales of 'W.W.' are set in the imaginary village of Claybury, which is largely based on Loughton. The thriller writer Ruth Rendell (b.1930) spent her early years in Loughton and set some of her first novels in the area. Sarah Flower Adams (1805-48) lived at Woodbury Hill; best known for composing the hymn *Nearer My God to Thee*, her finest work was her long dramatic poem *Vita Perpetua*. A less serious local writer was Sarah Martin (1768-1826), who wrote the nursery rhyme *Old Mother Hubbard*.

In the 17th century Lady Mary Wroth, of Loughton Hall, was one of the very first women authors in England. Her epic work *Urania* was a thinly-disguised satire on the royal court which scandalised high society. Nevertheless, she moved in a glittering social circle which included Ben Jonson and other leading writers of the day. The Wroth family, commemorated in the street-name Wroths Path, held Loughton Hall from 1579-1738, just one of several distinguished families of that manor.

Dick Turpin (1705-39), the notorious highwayman, made his mark in the area during his life of crime. In about 1734, the Widow Shelley, living on a farm on Traps Hill, was supposedly roasted over her own fire by Turpin until she confessed to where her money was hidden. In fact his last spell of 'going straight' before he became a professional thief appears to have been in Buckhurst Hill, where between 1733-4 he was a butcher. The area was no doubt convenient for deer-poaching, another of his 'trades'. Fear of his ruthless style of burglary led householders in Loughton to build 'Turpin traps', heavy wooden flaps let down over the top of the stairs and jammed in place with a pole against the upstairs ceiling. Some of these survived until the middle of the 19th century.

George Shillibeer (1799-1866), inventor of the omnibus, lived at Chigwell for many years, and now lies in its quiet churchyard.

83 Sir Eliab Harvey (1605-1698), *above left*. Sir Eliab began the Harvey family interest in Rolls Park, Chigwell, when he was bequeathed half the estate in 1668. The Harveys continued to own the estate until 1830. A nephew of William Harvey, the discoverer of the circulation of the blood, Sir Eliab, knighted at the Restoration for his support of the monarchy, was MP for Maldon until his death.

84 William Penn (1644-1718) *above*, founder of Pennsylvania, was brought up in Wanstead and spent his schooldays at Chigwell School. It was here that he had his first profound religious experience which in later life was to lead him to join the Quakers.

85 Thomas Fowell Buxton (1837-1916), *left*. The Buxton family had long connections with Essex and radical nonconformist causes. Thomas, with his brother Edward North Buxton, was a leading light in the preservation of Epping Forest, and was one of its first Verderers. He lived at Warlies, near Epping, and was prominent in social and charitable work in and around the Forest throughout his adult life.

86 Edward North Buxton (1840-1924), leading campaigner for the preservation of Epping Forest. He lived at Knightons, Buckhurst Hill, and was the leading light in the establishment of the Commons Preservation Society, and financed the Loughton Loppers' court case in 1866. Active in local politics and many philanthropic causes, he latterly became a Verderer of the Forest, and was instrumental in securing the preservation not only of Epping Forest but of Hainault Forest and Hatfield Forest too.

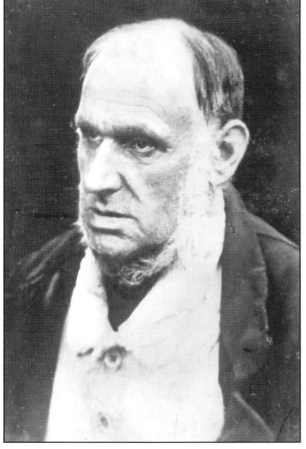

87 Samuel Willingale (1840-1911). Eldest son of old Thomas Willingale (1798-1870). The Willingale family's attempt to preserve their ancient rights to lop timber proved the turning point in saving Epping Forest from enclosure and destruction. After defiantly exercising his rights in 1866, Samuel was fined 2s. 6d., together with his cousins Alfred Willingale and William Higgins. All three went to jail rather than pay the fine, and public indignation at their treatment was instrumental in securing the Forest for the public.

88 Alfred Willingale (1843-1934) seen here in 1908, nephew of old Thomas Willingale. He was jailed in 1866 for lopping.

89 William Higgins (1842-70), nephew of old Thomas Willingale, also jailed in 1866 for lopping. He died at the young age of 28, only four years after being jailed, and descendants claimed this was as a delayed result of damp conditions in prison, where he caught a chill. This photograph dates from *c.*1862.

90 Thomas Willingale the Younger (1843-1925), second son of Old Thomas Willingale. He played no direct part in the lopping controversy, but his clothes are an excellent illustration of an Essex countryman's dress in the Edwardian period. Direct descendants of the Willingales still live in the area.

91 William Cole (1844-1922), prominent historian, of Buckhurst Hill. He was the founder, in 1880, of the Essex Field Club, and its Hon. Secretary from then until his death. The area spawned several other notable antiquarians. Isaac Chalkley Gould (1845-1907) lived in Traps Hill—an expert in prehistoric earthworks, he had an unrivalled knowledge of Essex topography, and was the first to excavate systematically the Red Hills (prehistoric salt mounds) of Essex. W.C. Waller (1850-1917), who lived at Ash Green, Loughton, wrote a monumental history of Loughton published in 1900 as *Loughton in Essex*.

92 Rev. William Dorling in 1880. He was, in 1868, the first minister of Buckhurst Hill Congregational Church, in Palmerston Road. Described as 'a man of strong character and advanced thought', he fell out with some of his congregation, who believed in eternal hellfire for those who were not practising nonconformists. Dorling was prepared to support a more generous admission ticket to heavenly bliss, so in 1871 he left and set up a rival establishment—Kings Place Independent Church—at the other end of Palmerton Road. Dorling was appointed pastor-for-life. Following his death in 1912, the building was sold to the Baptists, who still occupy the site today.

93 The Linder family, *c.*1893. The Linders were a prominent and prolific Buckhurst Hill family. Here they are assembled at their home, Oakhurst, built in 1929. Seated on the left is the founder of the dynasty, Samuel Linder (1812-1902). Linders Field in Roebuck Lane commemorates the family.

94 The 1862 parish choir of St John's, Buckhurst Hill, reassembled for this 1902 photograph. Pictured are (left to right): standing, G.H. Gussin (baker), Mr. Luffman (keeper), G.P. Clarke (schoolmaster, retired in 1905), F. Brand (organist—not in the 1862 choir), J. Greenaway (builder), H. Gussin (carpenter, died 1908), J. Bush (gardener); seated, S. Wilks (churchwarden, died 1908), P. Gellatly J.P., D.L. (verderer, chief warden), J. Whitaker Maitland (rector), and I.C. Colnett (curate—not in the 1862 choir).

95 An anonymous road worker, outside the Ash Green home of Loughton historian W.C. Waller, *c*.1905. Although a poor quality picture, it is rare to find such a photograph of working people going about their business.

Public Services

There was much civic pride in the local government of Chigwell and Loughton when the town hall was just a stroll away. Buckhurst Hill had been an Urban District in its own right since 1894, while Loughton achieved this status in 1900. Chigwell was rather more rural and retained parish status until 1933, when all three authorities joined together as Chigwell Urban District. This compact unit of local administration was, in 1974, merged with a number of other authorities to form Epping Forest District Council, with the new council's headquarters located in Epping. However, the wheel has now turned full circle as, following the 1994 Local Government Review, parish councils are to be set up in Buckhurst Hill, Chigwell and Loughton, so as to restore a measure of self-government at grassroots level.

Local government in England largely came about because of the need to improve local sanitation and sewage disposal, and even little Buckhurst Hill had its own sewage plant by 1876, ahead of Loughton. Buckhurst Hill had its own fire engine from 1884, once again ahead of provision in Loughton. Policing has, since 1840, been provided by the Metropolitan Police, with Loughton police station almost the furthest flung outpost of that force. The station was built in 1860, a solid and four-square building at the junction of High Road and Forest Road which survived until 1963, when it was rebuilt on a larger scale. Chigwell's modern police station was opened in Brook Parade in 1976.

Before the creation of universal health and welfare provision, there was much charitable work in the neighbourhood. Almshouses were established; Coulson's Almshouses in Chigwell, and the Whitaker Almshouses in Loughton. Buckhurst Hill's first village hospital opened in 1866, following a successful appeal for public subscriptions, and in Chigwell, Great West Hatch was run by a charitable institution (the Royal Eastern Counties Institution for Mental Defectives) until 1938. Best known of the charitable efforts in Loughton was the Shaftesbury Retreat, which allowed thousands of East End children to enjoy a day out in the Forest.

96 Following the creation of the unified Chigwell Urban District in 1933, a grand new town hall was built in Old Station Road, Loughton. Here, the building has been decorated for George VI's Coronation celebrations in 1937.

97 Buckhurst Hill's first post office, situated in the High Road opposite Holly House, was in use from 1862-83. The bay windows are a later addition. The building was later used as a milk shop.

98 After 1879, a purpose-built post office was opened at the top of Queen's Road, to be replaced with a larger office further down the road in 1892. Here we see post office staff assembled outside the office in 1914, the postmen smartly turned out in their shakos. Behind them, a sign gives details of National Service, an ominous echo of the distant guns of Flanders.

99 Forest Hospital was opened in Roebuck Lane, Buckhurst Hill, in 1912, replacing earlier hospitals in High Road and Knighton Lane. The building still stands.

100 Ratcliff Cottage, formerly The Red House, High Road, Buckhurst Hill. This building underwent a variety of uses, some of them charitable. It was first built in 1868, as the *Gold-diggers Arms*, reputedly by a miner returning from the Australian goldfields where had made his fortune. In 1872 it was purchased by local philanthropist Nathaniel Powell as a school to train working-class girls in domestic and laundry work. Later it was acquired by the 'Rescue Society for Girls', again training girls. From 1925 it was a cottage home for invalid and crippled children from Plaistow, until 1929 when it became a private house. Later it was in use as a youth hostel.

101 Chigwell U.D.C. fire service drill, *c.*1933. Buckhurst Hill's first (volunteer) fire brigade's first drill in 1885 was somewhat less successful. An attempt to extinguish an imaginary fire at Chigwell School resulted in bystanders getting more soaked than the school buildings, because of vandalism to the hoses. Despite this blow to their pride, the firemen were not too abashed to enjoy a good meat tea at the *King's Head* afterwards. Loughton's fire brigade had begun in *c.*1894.

102 This drinking fountain, a well-known Loughton landmark on the corner of Station Road and High Road, was erected *c*.1870, and is shown here *c*.1900. Holmehurst, the large house now forming part of Brown's car showrooms, can be seen in the background. The fountain was hit by a bus one foggy day in 1934, and rebuilt in timber on a rather less grand scale in 1936.

103 The Shaftesbury Retreat, Staples Road, Loughton. The Ragged School Union began arranging visits to the Forest by organised parties of poor East End children in 1891. Shortly afterwards, the Union changed its name to the Shaftesbury Society, and Loughton became the focus for their operations. Train-loads of children—with metal identity tags and locked into carriages—were brought on special trains in their thousands every summer, to be marched up Station Road and Forest Road to the Shaftesbury Retreat. The trains were paid for by Pearson's Fresh Air Fund, a charity promoted by a publishing magnate. The Retreat offered pony rides, funfair sideshows, a sit-down tea and a romp in the forest. Some local residents regarded the trips, which continued into the 1930s, as a nuisance, and local streets and parts of the forest were sprayed with disinfectant after the children had passed through! This house still stands.

104 The visit of the Prince of Wales and Princess Mary to Shaftesbury Retreat in 1921. Many famous people came to the retreat during its lifetime, to be seen publicly supporting its work. The grounds of the retreat have now been built over.

105　Local politics were as lively in the Edwardian period as they are now, and electioneering was perhaps even more striking then! This photograph shows Barclay Heward's Committee Room, Lynton Villa, Queen's Road, Buckhurst Hill. This was the home of Charles Linder, a prominent local Liberal. Heward stood in 1906 against Colonel Lockwood, the sitting Conservative member for the Epping Division. For the record, Heward lost!

Schools

Chigwell School, one of the oldest and foremost public schools in the country, was founded in 1629 by Samuel Harsnett, Archbishop of York, in gratitude for his spell as vicar of Chigwell from 1597-1605. A Latin School and English School were created, and the master of the Latin School was to be

> a graduate of one of the universities, not under twenty-seven years of age, a man skilful in the Greek and Latin tongues, a good Poet, of a sound religion, neither Papist nor Puritan, of a grave behaviour, of a sober and honest conversation, no tipler, nor Haunter of ale houses, no puffer of Tobacco, above all that he be apt to teach and severe in his government.

Speaking English in the Latin School was to be punishable by beating with a ferrule. Chigwell School's best-known pupil was William Penn (1644-1718), the founder of Pennsylvania. The affluence of the area has long attracted private schools such as Braeside and Oaklands; one of the largest was Loughton School, which originated as St John's College; there is a particular concentration in Buckhurst Hill.

Before the Education Act of 1870, apart from such private schools, the only provision for education was through the National Schools (run by the Church of England) and the British Schools (run by nonconformists). Chigwell had a National School by 1838, and in the same year a second was opened besides St John's Church, Buckhurst Hill. A British School was set up at Chigwell Row in the 1840s. Loughton's National School had its origins in a mid-18th-century church school, and a rival British School was established in Smart's Lane in about 1840. The Education Act required local authorities to put education on a proper footing, and school boards were set up in both Chigwell and Loughton and building programmes commenced.

The largest schools were the big secondary schools. Buckhurst Hill County High School for Boys, opened in 1938 on a prominent site beside Roding Lane, served as the boys' secondary school for the whole of the Chigwell Urban District. It has recently become a Sikh college. Loughton County High School for Girls was built, between 1908-1930 in Alderton Hill. Postwar developments have added further large secondary schools in Debden and at Grange Hill.

106 An engraving of the original Chigwell School, founded in 1629. This fine building is now the school library.

107 A 19th-century engraving of a schoolroom in Chigwell School. Nowadays classrooms are rather better appointed!

108 In this engraving of Chigwell School, boys are playing with a hoop outside the school. The Headmaster's house, added by Peter Burford in 1776, can be seen on the right, standing at right angles to the original building. A large extension was added to the rear in 1871.

109 Loughton National School, York Green. Built shortly after 1810, the school had to be expanded several times as the population grew; it was increased in size in 1834, 1842, 1863 and again in 1866. However, it was superseded by Staples Road School built nearby in 1887, and the National School ceased to function after 1911. The buildings were demolished in 1938-9 to make way for the Ashley Grove flats. York Green was sometimes known as School Green.

110 Staples Road School. The first board school in Loughton. Built as a boys' school in 1887, a girls' school was added as an extension on the west side. A separate infants, school was built to the east in 1891.

111 Loughton County High School for Girls, Alderton Hill. Opened in this building in 1908, the school had originated in a house in York Hill a couple of years before. The school was enlarged several times, including the addition of a new wing 1923-30. The building now forms the main campus for the Roding Valley High School.

Shops

Shopping is such an integral part of daily life it is hard to think of it as the stuff of social history. Yet the shops shown here portray lifestyles gone or vanishing. When were butchers no longer permitted to hang carcasses outside their premises? Whatever happened to Bateys, local maker of ginger beer and lemonade? When did milk stop being delivered by ladle from churns? Who remembers sugar sold in cones, wrapped in blue paper? Loose tea? Broken biscuits? Where did all the corn chandlers go? This selection offers a nostalgic look at a style of shopping that was altogether more leisurely than that seen in today's Loughton High Road.

Anciently, the nearest markets were at Epping and Waltham Abbey, and no doubt many villagers went to these place for produce. However, as Buckhurst Hill, Chigwell and Loughton grew, there were increasing demands for local services, and the number of shops grew too. However, even in the interwar years, Loughton High Road was a relatively small shopping centre, while Queen's Road, Buckhurst Hill and High Road, Chigwell, were smaller still. Local historian Dr. Donald Pohl recently undertook a remarkably detailed survey of Loughton life in 1851 from the census returns of that year. He noted five butchers, five bakers, eleven boot- and shoemakers (one grandly describing himself as a cordwainer), four tailors and 'innumerable' drapers and grocers. There was also one stationer, situated on York Hill. Quite an impressive array of shops for a village with a population of only 1,237, and no doubt reflecting the area's relative affluence.

One of the most striking things about shopping today in the area is how modern the shops are. There are scarcely any pre-war shop buildings in Loughton High Road, particularly at the north end, and Chigwell's shopping focus has shifted from the area around the parish church to the modern Brook Parade further south. Only in Buckhurst Hill does the main shopping street, Queen's Road, retain much of its older charm. There has been much public debate in recent years about the future of shopping in the three villages; the growth of 'out of town' superstores has seemed to threaten the vitality of local shopping centres. However, it seems likely that there will always be room for near-at-hand stores, and the main shopping streets, bustling with life, have all the appearance of thriving foci for community life.

112 Looking up Queen's Road, Buckhurst Hill, *c*.1910. On the corner are Sapsford's confectioner's, and, with the car outside, Cosson's the stationer's.

113 Metson's clothing shop, Queen's Road, Buckhurst Hill, 1912. A splendid array of gentlemen's togs. Metson's remained in business until 1983.

114 Interior of a Queen's Road shoe shop, before the First World War. This is an unusual image as photographs of shop interiors at this date are relatively rare.

115 International Stores, Queen's Road, 1915, with the staff standing outside, including the delivery boy!

116 Harris the Butcher, Queen's Road, with a donkey cart from the Buckhurst Hill Pig Club outside. This photograph dates from *c*.1916, when such pig and rabbit clubs were very common ways of increasing the short supply of meat. Between the wars, the proprietor Sandy Harris was a well-known Buckhurst Hill character. The livestock was, until the Second World War, brought on the hoof to the shop to be slaughtered on the premises. The shop is still a butcher's.

117 A bookstall on Buckhurst Hill station, 1903. The fascinating news headlines on the hoarding note a small revolution in Venezuela, a royal visit to Malta, and the impending F.A. Cup Final.

118 Clinch, grocer's and draper's of Chigwell Row, *c*.1910.

119 Davis' stationery shop, Loughton High Road, decorated for Queen Victoria's Diamond Jubilee in 1897. Flags, Chinese lanterns and fairy lights complement a patriotic display in the shop window.

120 Bosworth's butcher's shop, Church Hill, 1910. A striking display of meat! Bosworth's are the oldest family firm still trading in Loughton, having been founded in 1886. The shop was largely rebuilt in 1906. The premises above once housed the reading room of the Loughton Institute, but in the rebuilt shop they were converted into accommodation.

121 An advertisement for Hazlewood's butcher's in 1896. Bosworth's once had many rivals, but today there is only one other butcher trading in Loughton High Road.

122 Green's cycle shop, Loughton High Road, *c.*1902. Cycling was an immensely popular pastime when roads were less busy than they are now, and weekends and bank holidays would find the roads from London to Epping Forest bustling with cyclists. Cycling Clubs, of which there were many, would frequently arrange special day-trips to the forest. The fancy has not entirely disappeared; anyone frequenting the forest today will often have had their reveries disturbed by lycra-clad groups of mud-spattered cyclists hurtling out of thickets on multi-geared mountain bikes.

123　The Loughton branch of the Co-op, *c.*1912.

124 Goodall's, the baker's in 1916. This shop was situated opposite St Mary's Church in the High Road.

125 Debden Broadway, built in 1958 to serve as the shopping focus of the Debden estate. At least one architectural critic has been emphatically unkind about this parade; Norman Scarfe, writing in the *Shell Guide to Essex*, called it 'unspeakably nasty in scale and in entire conception!'

Social Life

The Chigwell and Loughton area has for a century had an immensely rich social life, with a vast array of clubs, institutes and societies. In the past, this social activity was co-ordinated by a benevolent oligarchy of wealthy men and women who lived in the areas's big houses and who pursued their leisure interests in natural history, antiquarianism, charitable works or sporting activities with astonishing fervour and dedication. Before the area was built up, the churches and inns provided what social activity there was, supplemented by traditional rural celebrations such as the Easter Hunt in the Forest, the Horkey feast after harvest home, and a considerable amount of drinking at forest lopping time in November. A hiring fair in Chigwell held during the 19th century no doubt included much socialising.

Loughton itself was something of a tourist resort in the Victorian and Edwardian periods, when—together with Chingford—it was the main destination for East Enders making their way to the Forest. The regular arrival of vast numbers of East Londoners caused some friction locally, and there were regular complaints about the unhygienic ways of the visitors leading to sanitary problems for the civic authorities; not for nothing was Loughton nicknamed, 'Lousy Loughton!' However, for others, the hordes of trippers passing through the town provided both an entertaining spectacle and a ready source of revenue.

The cultural pursuits of the area are manifold. Loughton Operatic Society celebrated its centenary in 1994, one of the oldest in the Home Counties, while there are a host of younger but equally lively amateur dramatic societies. Women's Institutes and Townswomen's Guilds thrive. The Chigwell and Loughton History Society was founded in 1962 and is well-supported, while its older sisters the Essex Archaeological Society (founded in 1852, now the Essex Society for Archaeology and History) and the Essex Field Club were virtually dependent during their early years on the amateur scholarship and dedication of men and women from Buckhurst Hill, Chigwell and Loughton. In Loughton, the Lopping Hall forms a natural focus for social life, while Loughton Hall in Debden has long been used by community associations. Residents' Associations are strongly supported, and the largest of them returns several members to the local council. Politics and social life have been closely mixed in the past; in the 19th century, the Anglican churches were bastions of Conservatism, while nonconformist chapels tended to favour the Liberal cause. Both church and chapel established rival social activities. This in Loughton in 1892, there were two cricket clubs, two brass bands, and two temperance leagues, each mutually exclusive.

The open spaces of the area have encouraged sporting activities to flourish. There are golf clubs at both Chigwell and Loughton. Buckhurst Hill Cricket Club, with its ground next to Powell's Forest, is one of the oldest in the county, having been founded in 1864, while Loughton Cricket Club meets at the ground beside Traps Hill once known as Mott's Croft. In Chigwell, the Epping Forest Country Club, and Police Metropolitan Sports Club both occupy historic buildings and offer a wide range of modern sporting activities, while the David Lloyd's Sports Club is built on part of the former site of RAF Chigwell.

126 Loughton schoolchildren enjoying the traditional May Festival in 1903; the May Queen is surrounded by her attendants.

127 A stirring tug-of-war contest at Buckhurst Hill village sports day in 1913.

128 The swimming-pool at Grange Farm, Chigwell. This facility was established in October 1951 by Princess Elizabeth (now H.M. the Queen) to benefit the residents of Epping Forest as a recreational and educational resource. Swimming was only one of a wide range of leisure activities at Grange Farm, until it became a camp-site in 1973. This closed in 1984, and the site is now (1995) derelict.

129 The Corbett Theatre, Rectory Lane, in 1973. This is the home of the E15 Acting School, originally established at Stratford's Theatre Royal by Joan Littlewood. The building is a converted barn brought to Loughton from Sussex, and is host to a wide range of amateur dramatic and operatic functions.

130 Loughton High Road, 1897. A monumental arch erected to celebrate Queen Victoria's Diamond Jubilee. It stood approximately at what is now the junction with The Drive.

131 The various forest retreats—places offering non-alcoholic refreshment to visitors and trippers—were also popular with local people out for a walk. This is Vale Retreat, Forest Road, in 1903. Advertised as 'The Cyclists' Rest', tea was offered at 3d., while hot water, for those bringing their own screws of tea, was a mere 2d.

132   A ladies' charabanc outing from the *Carpenters' Arms*, Loughton, *c*.1919.

133   And the men went too! Buttonholed and behatted, another charabanc outing from the *Carpenters' Arms*, *c*.1919.

134 Loughton Cinema in 1928 in the High Road, shortly after it opened. In this view, the post office can be seen a few doors further along. The cinema is showing the Hitchcock film *The Farmer's Wife*, and also advertising an otherwise-forgotten western, *Raiders of the Dark*. The cinema was demolished in 1963 to make way for a new parade of shops. Note the vacant plot next to the cinema; even as late as 1928 there was undeveloped land in central Loughton.

135 A float from the Loughton Poultry & Rabbit Club, taking part in the 1937 Jubilee Parade.

Streets

The Roman road from London to Great Dunmow ran through what is now Chigwell, close to the route now followed by the High Road. Evidence of the road has been painstakingly uncovered at Abridge by the West Essex Archaeological Group.

Loughton's High Road in the Middle Ages ran to Woodford to the south, but to the north, surrounded by Forest, it petered out, with footpaths running down to the Roding from Buckhurst Hill and to Chigwell. However, between 1611-22, the High Road was extended via what is now Church Hill and Golding's Hill to Epping, and this quickly became the main coaching route from London to East Anglia. However, the steep hills made it a difficult route for horse-drawn traffic, so in 1830-34 the Epping New Road was constructed. As early as 1404 the High Road was mentioned in a court action, when one John Lucteborough was prosecuted for throwing the rubbish from his ditch outside Richard Algor's gate on the King's highway. Richard Algor's house survived in part, concealed by much overbuilding, until 1963 near the junction of Algers Road and High Road.

Although many of Loughton's other roads are of ancient origin, such as Rectory Lane, Traps Hill, and Smart's Lane, the smaller side-streets are relative newcomers, with (very roughly), the west side of the High Road being developed from about 1881 up to the First World War, and the east side largely being built up in the Edwardian and interwar periods.

Buckhurst Hill's development was spurred on by the arrival of the railway, and the main routes were laid out east-west from the station to the High Road, with a further estate east of the railway (Albert Road etc.) laid out in 1856-60.

So the development of the road network in Chigwell, Buckhurst Hill and Loughton parallels the growth of the villages themselves. Chigwell's road pattern has changed least of all, as Chigwell has remained largely rural. Gravel Lane, Green Lane and Pudding Lane are descriptive names of very ancient routes. Manor Road, now lined with substantial and elegant homes, was such a muddy track in 1817 that it was not counted a public highway. The curious kink in the road around Rolls Park, where Chigwell High Road becomes Abridge Road, was the work of the powerful Harvey family, owners of Rolls Park, who diverted the road in the 18th century to enable them to extend their grounds.

136 Looking down Loughton High Road from King's Green, *c*.1877. On the left, Monghyr Cottage can be seen at the corner of Traps Hill. This elegant early 19th-century house was for a time the home of prominent architect James Cubitt, and after a period of neglect, has recently been restored and converted into offices. The large houses on the right no longer exist, having been replaced with a modern parade of shops.

137 This 1890s view of Loughton High Road was taken outside the *Crown*. The white picket fence of Sadler's Livery stables can be seen on the right, while on the other side of the road, two ladies pose with their baby-carriages, and a policeman regards the scene impassively. The great bulk of Lopping Hall dominates the skyline.

138 Loughton High Road in 1901. Blow's bakery stands on the right, with the village post office and telephone exchange beyond it, at the junction with Forest Road. Most of the buildings survive. The substantial brick building beyond is the first Loughton police station, built between 1860-64, and replaced in 1963. Blow's horse-drawn delivery vans are ready to set off on their rounds.

139 This unusual triangular block at the junction of Smart's Lane and High Beech Road has recently been flattened to make way for a car park. Smart's Lane, on the right, is an ancient route into the forest, and was earlier known as Allards Lane. This name, like Ollards Grove nearby, is derived from a 14th-century resident, Edward Athelard. The name was changed to commemorate Matthew Smart, who owned a cottage in the lane in 1819.

140 Loughton High Road, *above left*, was flooded in 1926. Here a car gingerly steers round the surface water outside Allison's Granaries.

141 Looking down York Hill, *c.*1877, *left*. The weatherboarded building on the left is Tile Kiln Farm. The farm name is a reminder of the tile-making industry carried out nearby. York Hill itself was earlier known as Mutton Row, a joking reference to 'black mutton' or poached venison which could easily be obtained in the 18th and 19th centuries from the adjacent forest. The name York Hill commemorates a scandalous affair between Frederick, Duke of York, and a local actress and socialite, Mary Anne Clarke (1776-1852), who lived at Loughton Lodge nearby.

142 The same view as in illustration 141, but half a century later, *above*. This photograph was taken on 10 June 1929, and considerable changes have taken place. York Hill and Staples Road to the right, have been made up, and Tile Kiln Farm has become a derelict adjunct of a furniture shop. A small boy stands in Queen's Park (later Queens) Road, under an advertisement for the Ilford Super Cinema, which that week was showing *Happiness Ahead* and *She's A Good Girl*. The shop remains to this day, though Tile Kiln Farm has been demolished, and the shop opposite (advertising Hudson's Soap and Zebo grate lead) has become a private house. The tea garden on the corner of Staples Road has now been partly built over, but part remains as the beer garden of the *Wheatsheaf*.

143 This utterly rural scene, *below*, would be quite unrecognisable today. Taken from the corner of Carroll Hill, the view is down Church Lane, then just a track between open fields. The photograph was taken on 18 March 1929.

144 Rectory Lane in June 1895, *right*, near what is now the junction with Pyrles Lane. This area was then known as Parson's or Rectory Green, as the parish rectory stood at the junction. It is claimed that the fencing visible in the middle distance is a relic of one of the original clap-gates by which the Forest was enclosed in earlier days.

145 The 'Uplands' estate in the course of development, July 1904, *below right*. This estate was laid out east of Church Hill following the demolition of a large house called *Uplands* in 1901. In this view, looking up Church Hill, Bosworth's butcher's shop stands on the left, with new houses of the Uplands Estate being completed on the right. A horse and cart passes in front of the brick piers of 1 Church Hill (also known as *Uplands*—now Loughton Montessori Nursery), and obscures the entrance to Uplands Park Avenue (now simply called The Uplands). One of the two fine cedar trees survives, but the magnificent tulip tree, which formed part of the ornamental grounds of Uplands, has disappeared.

146 Forest Road, *c*.1900, at the junction of Staples Road (on the left) and Smart's Lane (on the right). The white fence in Staples Road marks the little bridge over Loughton Brook. This junction was no doubt the reason for Smart's Lane being known locally as Wonks Way; *wonks*, or more correctly *wantz* is an Essex dialect word usually applied to a road leading to a junction.

147 A snowy Church Hill, Loughton, *c*.1890, *left*.

148 Englands Lane, Loughton, in 1895, *right*, looking towards Debden Green. This area was built up in the 1920s. Named after one George England, who owned a house hereabouts in 1648, it was earlier known as Ree Lane, from the Old English word for water; a stream still runs under Englands Lane near its junction with Clay Lane, and at one time this was a frequently-flooded ford.

149 Golding's Hill, Loughton, *c.*1898. This road was constructed between 1611-22 to link Loughton to Epping, and raised onto an embankment to lessen its steepness in 1774. The large open space known as Arewater Green stands to the left of the horse and gig, while Lower Road is on the right. The writer W.W. Jacobs (1863-1943) lived in a house on Golding's Hill from about 1910 to his death.

150 The Debden estate under construction. This huge estate was built up after 1945 by the London County Council, following the sale of 644 acres, including Loughton Hall, by Commander J.W. Maitland. The Maitland family had owned the estate since 1825. Rectory Lane can be seen running across the centre of the photograph, with Debden Broadway threading across the top of the picture.

151 Pyrles Lane, Debden. A shopping parade erected as part of the Debden estate, with the post office behind the oak tree on the right. Many mature trees like the two in this photograph were retained during the building of the estate to add character to the new environment.

152　Borders Lane, *c*.1905, near the junction with Alderton, Spareleaze and Traps Hill.

153　Borders Lane after its redevelopment as part of the Debden estate. Borders Farm was demolished during the building work.

154 Chigwell New Road, now Roding Lane, in May 1906. This road was built by Mr. Arthur Savill (of Savill's estate agents) in 1890 to replace the footpath between Buckhurst Hill and Chigwell; this crossed at White Bridge and was frequently impassable because of flooding.

155 High Road, Chigwell, looking at the west side of the street on 25 August 1936. A fine view of Chigwell 'village' centre between the wars. The entrance to Radley's builder's yard stands between 'Dawkins', once a shop, and 'Radley Cottage'. Radley's is still in business.

156 An undated postcard view of Vicarage Lane, Chigwell, looking south from near Oaks Farm. This is a very ancient road, once gated at the Forest end to keep out deer and cattle, and recorded as early as 1492 as *Wycaryes Lane*.

157 A postcard of Queen's Road, Buckhurst Hill. This remains Buckhurst Hill's main shopping thoroughfare, built in 1856-7. Knighton Lane runs off to the right, past the Essex Cycle Co. shop. Knighton Lane was locally known as Hospital Lane as the village hospital once stood there. The stationery shop on the left is now a newsagent's.

158 Council houses in Brook Road, Buckhurst Hill, 1925. Brook Road, formerly Barn Lane, which leads to Chingford, is part of the area known as West Buckhurst Hill, i.e. that part of Buckhurst Hill lying west of the Epping New Road. This view looks west towards Chingford; just out of sight stands Riggs Retreat, one of the best known of the many Forest refreshment rooms, which operated from 1879-1969 despite several catastrophic fires. The site is now a caravan park.

159 Palmerston Road, Buckhurst Hill, *c.*1903. Formerly a rough track known as Heath Row—this appellation taken from a local builder with the delightful name of Comfort Heath—Palmerston Road was first made up in 1868, together with Gladstone and Westbury Roads. In this view we are looking up the road near what is now King's Avenue. A signboard on the left announces 'freehold land to be sold'.

160 These charming redbrick villas stand in Staples Road, Loughton. Named Clara, Edith, Ellen and Louisa Villas, they reputedly take their names from the four daughters of the builder. First made up in 1865, Staples Road takes its name from Staple Hill, part of the Forest which lies immediately opposite these houses. This hill was the traditional meeting place of the Loughton Loppers, and the name is an ancient one; *stapol* is Old English for marker post.

161 The Old White Bridge, *c.*1900. Before the construction of Roding Lane, this was the main route between Buckhurst Hill and Chigwell!

Transport

The railway first came to Loughton in 1856, when the Eastern Counties Railway (later the Great Eastern) opened a branch line via Woodford. This was extended in 1865 to Ongar. The loop line from Leytonstone to Woodford which takes in, *inter alia*, Hainault, Grange Hill, Chigwell and Roding Valley stations, was opened in 1903. After the Second World War, these services were electrified in stages and handed to London Transport's Central Line. Electrification was completed as far as Loughton on 21 November 1948 (including the loop line), with the section to Epping completed on 26 September 1949. After years of decline, the final section of this line, from Epping to Ongar, was closed in 1994. The arrival of the railway was undoubtedly a key factor in the development of the area, particularly in Buckhurst Hill, and also provided visitors with a convenient and cheap way of reaching Epping Forest, transforming it into the 'East Enders' Playground'.

Before the railways, there were regular stagecoaches from Chigwell and Loughton to London, and Epping New Road was an important stagecoach route through to Cambridge, Norwich, and other East Anglian towns. Direct omnibus services linked Loughton to London from 1915. The old No.10 route from Victoria—Abridge has long disappeared, but the No.20 service—now run by Grey-Green, from Walthamstow—Epping survives, though much truncated.

Buckhurst Hill was, for a short time, the site for an unusual tramway experiment. A 600 metre track was laid through Lord's Bushes as a trial run for a new tramway system for Lisbon. The railway had a single central metal rail, with two timber supporting beams running parallel. A single steam locomotive, the *Cintra* ran up and down this miniature line, hauling delighted local schoolchildren in two small carriages. The experimental runs operated between 1872 and 1873, after which time the locomotives were shipped to Portugal and the line removed, though a sandy path through the woods still marks the route. Ironically, the Lisbon venture failed, and the line never opened.

162 Loughton's first railway station was opened on 22 August 1856 and stood on the site now occupied by Lopping Hall. There was a turntable where the drinking fountain in High Road now stands, and sidings over the later site of St Mary's Church. After the 1865 extension to Epping, a replacement station was built on the alignment of the new line further south. This photograph shows that second station, *c*.1903. A line of horse cabs stands ready, and the goods sidings can be seen beyond the station; these sidings stand on the former route to the earlier station. In the distance are open fields, now Tycehurst Hill and Spareleaze Hill.

163 Loughton station staff, *c*.1903. No fewer than 19 men proudly display their G.E.R. uniforms.

164 In the late 1930s, Loughton station was rebuilt further east in a striking architectural style with boldly curving concrete canopies echoing the curvature of the line itself as it passes through the station, while the booking-office below the embankment is of almost monumental proportions in yellow brick, the main hall being lit by a single large half-moon window. This photograph, taken from the footbridge leading to Algers Road, shows the old station being demolished in 1940, with the new station in the distance.

165 This snowy scene dating from 1963 was taken from Loughton station looking up the line towards London.

166   Though the canopy and distinctive name-board have gone, little else had changed at Buckhurst Hill station since this photograph was taken at the turn of the century.

167   Debden station was earlier known as Chigwell Lane. This photograph shows the down-platform buildings shortly before rebuilding work in 1973.

168   The up-platform at Debden station, shortly before its demolition in 1973.

169 The impressive railway viaduct over the Roding carrying the loop line to Chigwell and beyond, *above left*. The small footbridge in the foreground was once the only link between Buckhurst Hill and Chigwell; it connected Luxborough Lane to what is now Lower Queen's Road. A road bridge was not built until 1890, when Roding Lane was opened.

170 In this 1929 photograph, *left*, an L.N.E.R. train has left Loughton station and is en route to Epping.

171 A G.E.R. parcels van on Alderton Hill, *c.*1903, *above*.

SADLER & SONS,

HIGH ROAD, LOUGHTON

(Near the Loughton Station),

LICENSED TO LET

OPEN PHAETONS, BROUGHAMS, FLYS, WAGGONETTES

PONY AND BASKET CHAISES,

AND

CARRIAGES OF EVERY DESCRIPTION.

HORSES CLIPPED & SINGED ON APPROVED PRINCIPLES

NEW LIVERY YARD,

(NEAR THE "CROWN" HOTEL AND PUBLIC HALL).

CORN, FLOUR & SEED MERCHANTS.

172 Sadler's was one of Loughton's largest livery stables. This photograph shows the yard, *c.*1906. The *Crown* can be seen on the extreme right.

173 An 1896 advertisement for Sadler's stables.

War

Buckhurst Hill, Chigwell and Loughton have all played their part in the two World Wars, and many young men who went out from the three villages did not return to their families. In Loughton a cross on King's Green lists the names of the fallen, while Buckhurst Hill's dead are commemorated on the lych gate of St John's. In Chigwell a carved oak memorial screen in the south aisle was unveiled in 1920, and a rough-hewn Celtic cross stands outside inscribed with 63 names of Chigwell's fallen. Five years later, a memorial chapel was dedicated at Chigwell School to former pupils who fell in the Great War.

During the First World War, anti-aircraft positions were located in Epping Forest as part of the wider defences of London, but action was minor compared to the Second World War. There are, however, residents still alive who recall hearing the Silvertown explosion in 1917, when a TNT factory in the Royal Docks blew up killing 73 people. The sound of the blast could be heard from The Wash to Brighton.

On the very first day of the Blitz, 7 September 1940 (Black Saturday), a Hurricane from 303 Squadron crashed onto an air-raid shelter in Roding Road, killing three occupants. The Polish pilot baled out, and was promptly arrested as he could speak virtually no English. Also killed by 'friendly fire' was PC Albert Hinds, blown up outside Loughton Police Station by a shell from an anti-aircraft battery in Nursery Road. Two A.R.P men nearby died later from their injuries. Even before the Blitz had begun, there was sporadic German bombing; two people were killed in The Drive on 26 July 1940, the first fatalities of the war in the London Civil Defence Region. In a raid of 1941 farms in Loughton and Debden were damaged, while a gun battery at Loughton Hall was hit, killing a soldier. At Staples Road School the white-painted air-raid shelter directions are still clearly visible:

CASUALTY ENTRANCE ➜THROUGH AIRLOCK BY SANDBAGS.

Buckhurst Hill, a very small parish, was nevertheless hit by a total of about fifty high-explosive bombs, six fire-bombs, six parachute mines, two oil-bombs, and unfortunately, no less than 30 anti-aircraft shells from nearby batteries. The worst night was 18-19 March 1941, when a number of houses received direct hits and the *Prince Alfred* tavern was demolished.

The area received large numbers of refugees both during the Phoney War and during the Blitz. These did not include schoolchildren, who were sent further afield, but did include refugees fleeing Nazi rule in Europe and East Enders who had had their homes destroyed by bombing. Chigwell alone had 1,000 refugees to accommodate. However, the proximity of the Forest made self-sufficiency easier than for many city-dwellers. There were numerous rabbit clubs and pig co-operatives; these latter gathered bracken and acorn from the Forest to provide bedding and food for their beasts, while women's institutes were busy each summer gathering elder-flowers for cordials and jam. The Forest itself was also important as a holiday venue; to maintain morale a 'Holidays at Home' scheme encouraged the use of such places for economical breaks, and during the summer months numerous entertainments were staged in the area. In Chigwell on 19 April 1941 a parachute mine demolished the *Prince of Wales*, a telephone exchange and nearby cottages. Forty-two died in that raid. The construction of R.A.F. Chigwell from 1937 onwards resulted in the demolition of Chigwell Hall. R.A.F. Chigwell was home to 4 Balloon Centre which flew barrage balloons as part of London's defences, and later it was also host to a radar unit. The base remained operational until 1958 and, having reverted back to nature, now forms part of the Roding Valley Meadows nature reserve.

174   Loughton celebrates the end of the Boer War in 1902. A small band halts on Church Hill, flanked by two serious-looking policemen. Behind them is a patriotic flock of schoolchildren clutching a forest of Union Flags, while local people, many turned out in Sunday best, look on.

175   Buckhurst Hill Church Lads' Brigade undergoing military training during the First World War.

176   Loughton's war memorial on King's Green commemorates the 92 men of the parish who fell in the Great War. The monument was unveiled by Lord Lambourne in 1920. This photograph, taken *c.*1925, shows an NS type bus with A.E.C. chassis, one of the first covered top buses in general use, working route No.100 as it passes the *King's Head*. Next door stands Salmon's 'Loughton Refreshment Rooms', today an accountants' office.

177 A morale-boosting military parade down Forest Road, Loughton, in 1918. Loughton post office stands on the extreme right.

178 Braeside, a girls' public school in Buckhurst Hill High Road, was turned into a nursing-home during the First World War. Here nurses pose with wounded soldiers.